This book belongs to

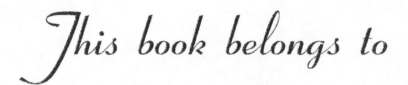

LOVER OF FLEA MARKETS

GRAPHIC DESIGN ADAPTED FROM MID-TWENTIETH CENTURY SCREEN-PRINTED TABLECLOTH

EDITORIAL STAFF

Vice President and Editor-in-Chief: Sandra Graham Case. *Executive Director of Publications:* Cheryl Nodine Gunnells. *Special Projects Design Director:* Patricia Uhiren. *Graphic Artist:* Dale Rowett. *Publications Director:* Kristine Anderson Mertes. *Editorial Director:* Susan Frantz Wiles. *Photography Director:* Lori Ringwood Dimond. *Art Operations Director:* Jeff Curtis. TECHNICAL — *Managing Editor:* Leslie Schick Gorrell. *Book Coordinator:* Jean W. Lewis. *Senior Technical Writer:* Stacey Robertson Marshall. *Technical Writers:* Christina Price Kirkendoll, Shawnna B. Manes, Barbara Marguerite McClintock, Kimberly J. Smith, and Theresa Hicks Young. EDITORIAL — *Managing Editor:* Alan Caudle. *Senior Associate Editor:* Susan McManus Johnson. DESIGN ASSISTANTS — Lisa Curton, Karla Edgar, Joyce Holland, and Amy Pritts. ART — *Art Publications Director:* Rhonda Shelby. *Art Imaging Director:* Mark Hawkins. *Art Category Manager:* Lora Puls. *Lead Graphic Artist:* Dana Vaughn. *Graphic Artist:* Matt Davis. *Imaging Technician:* Stephanie Johnson. *Staff Photographer:* Russell Ganser. *Publishing Systems Administrator:* Becky Riddle. *Publishing Systems Assistants:* Clint Hansen, Myra S. Means, and Chris Wertenberger. PROMOTIONS — *Associate Editor:* Steven M. Cooper. *Graphic Artist:* Deborah Kelly.

BUSINESS STAFF

Publisher: Rick Barton. *Vice President, Finance:* Tom Siebenmorgen. *Director of Corporate Planning and Development:* Laticia Mull Cornett. *Vice President, Retail Marketing:* Bob Humphrey. *Vice President, Sales:* Ray Shelgosh. *Vice President, National Accounts:* Pam Stebbins. *Director of Sales and Services:* Margaret Reinold. *Vice President, Operations:* Jim Dittrich. *Comptroller, Operations:* Rob Thieme. *Retail Customer Service Managers:* Sharon Hall and Stan Raynor. *Print Production Manager:* Fred F. Pruss.

Made in the United States of America

Library of Congress Control Number 2002113493
Hardcover ISBN 1-57486-275-8
Softcover ISBN 1-57486-276-6

10 9 8 7 6 5 4 3 2

EASY FLEA MARKET STYLE

6

Introduction

8

Discover the fun of flea market style! Plan your kitchen décor around the beauty of old crates. Let ladders put everything within easy reach. And snap up vintage cameras for photo frames that will make you smile. Do it all in a flash with Fabulous Finds like these!

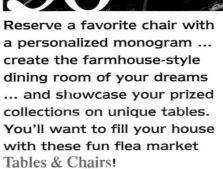
CONTENTS

"All true civilization is ninety

an accumulation of small

left by the countless generations

62

Jewelry sparkles on the dining table, twinkles from elegant cushions, and shines on lampshades. Let flea market riches refine and define Your Treasured Home. After all, you deserve these quick little luxuries!

74

Tarnished brassware can shine anew, no polishing needed! Learn the easy techniques to perk up old planters, revive a decorative bowl, and liven up old lamps. We think you'll agree — these beautiful accessories are nothing less than Top Brass.

84

Revitalize flea market lamps or create your own using collectibles like decanters, jars, tins, — even shoes! Whether you're an avid flea market fan or just getting started, Illuminations will have you seeing lamps in a whole new light.

per cent heirlooms and memories —
but precious deposits
that have gone before us." —Robert I Gannon, S.J.

96

Routine castoffs recycled into romantic candleholders? Yes! These sweet transformations celebrate the Romance of Candles. Butter dishes, ashtrays, chandeliers, and other unexpected flea market items go from run-of-the-mill to radiant in just minutes.

108

Baskets, candles in collectible holders, and new ways to present flowers — for extraordinary gift ideas, look no further than the flea market. Gifted Giving is a knack that's easily learned. Surprise someone special with these fun presentations!

122

Make the most of long summer days with these quick and easy ways to enjoy the great outdoors. Find new uses for old pots and pans. Beat the heat with flea market coolers. And pep up your houseplants with cheery planters. Do it all with Alfresco Style.

CONTENTS

"I just <u>love</u> *old stuff* ... Don't you?"

For me, strolling the aisles of a flea market can encompass many emotions. Nostalgia, when I see something that reminds me of my Grandma Velda's house. Surprise, when I turn the corner and see the very thing I have been searching for, lo, these many months! Excitement, when I see the wonderful possibility in a forlorn treasure that's waiting for a second chance. And fear, that my new find will not fit in my car!

The biggest thrill, though, is blending these flea market treasures into my home décor. It's usually very simple and quick to do, and this book is filled with easy, exciting ideas and inspiration to help you create your own flea market style. Be inventive. Be creative. Think about using old things in unexpected new ways. For example, who would have thought an old pocketbook (page 86) could be transformed into a romantic, feminine lamp? Or that a stack of bowls (page 127) could become a fun and useful table?

In your flea market explorations, don't overlook the common, everyday items like canning jars, old jewelry, or mismatched punch cups. They can become thoughtful gifts or fun accessories that don't cost a fortune.

Enjoy the rediscovered neat stuff in this book. Be inspired by the things you love, and you'll be on your way to your own flea market style. Remember, that next treasure is just waiting around the corner!

Patti

Patricia Uhiren, Special Projects Design Director

FABULOUS FINDS

Flea market shopping is fun!
No matter what you find —
old canning jars, kitchen
drawers, even ladders — you
have the basis for a quick
home décor project. The ideas
on the following pages are your
invitation to fall in love with
the ease of flea market style.
Find a project that inspires you
to make something fabulous!

Now in living color:
Tune in to the renewed
beauty of an old TV
stand. Our combed
cabinet (page 138)
puts on a show in the
kitchen by hosting an
assortment of favorite
collectibles while
providing the scoop on
coffee beans. The
cabinet's unique paint
finish and fabric panels
are an easy makeover
program that's sure to
win rave reviews.

FIND *Fabulous*

It's all within your reach...

...especially when you use a ladder! If you need to organize a lot of items in a small space, think vertical. A ladder is great for elevating everything from egg beaters to bath lotions. Check garage sales as well as flea markets for these upwardly mobile decorating accessories.

Baskets transform this castoff ladder into a hardworking clutter-catcher. We used wire-edged cotton ribbon to tie the baskets to the rungs.

Proving its versatility, the same ladder goes from kitchen to bath. The rungs now hold towels, a magazine rack, a wire basket, and a miniature washtub.

A CASE

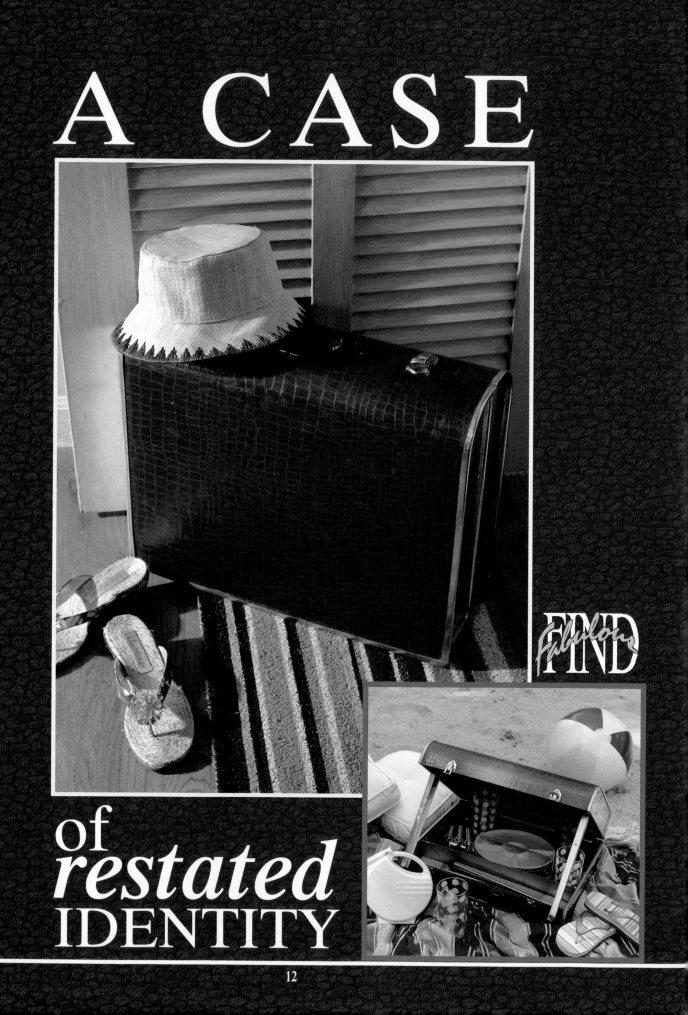

Fabulous FIND

of *restated* IDENTITY

Dining alfresco? Don't forget your luggage! Who knew that this 20th century valise is actually a picnic table, complete with dinnerware inside? The fold-out legs snap into place, converting the aluminum-framed case into an Instant tabletop. A sheet of tempered glass makes a regular fixture of this portable find.

CRATE
Centerpieces

Farmhouse charm packs a "crate" deal of style. Some flea market ideas are so easy — and so *right* — you wonder why you never thought of them before. Old-fashioned egg and produce crates lend themselves to many uses, but have you ever considered them as easy centerpieces for your table? Here are three lighthearted, lovely, and creative ways to use … crates!

Above and opposite, top left: Gather berry baskets into a handled berry flat ... these flowers look almost as yummy as the original cargo.

Opposite, top right: There's a whole garden of artificial veggies growing in this asparagus crate.

Opposite, below: Ceramic roosters find something to crow about while this old egg crate blooms with silk flowers.

"Beauti-fool" Flowers

There's simply no improving on a bouquet of Nature's sweet blossoms ... or is there? Can you tell which of these arrangements in flea market jars is a gathering of fool-the-eye silk blossoms? Believe it or not, all of these "fresh" cut flowers are artificial and so is the crystal-clear "water"! You can purchase the floral arranging resin from craft or home decorating stores and make an everlasting silk bouquet of your own.

Fabulous FIND

Clear floral arranging resin hardens as it cures, so you never have to wipe up spills!

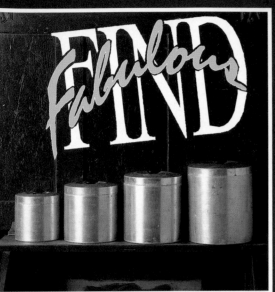

FABULOUS FIND

LITTLE KITCHEN HELPERS

There's no containing the excitement — metal canisters are truly fabulous finds! Leave them plain to show off their brushed aluminum finish, or use paint to give your storage set retro charm. Just tape off the knobs on the containers and spray on a coat of primer. Paint the dry canisters with green acrylic paint. Sand lightly with fine sandpaper to reveal the paint underneath and create an aged look. For labels, photocopy the designs, page 152. Cut out the labels and adhere them to the canisters. Your set is complete!

We used a vintage tablecloth to top the lid of this fun cookie tin — without cutting up the cloth! Want to know the secret? Turn to page 139 for instructions and label pattern. It's just uncanny!

Table Service

Gather all your dining necessities — condiments, napkins, and dishes — into a flea market caddy that can go from shelf to table in seconds. This little caddy is actually a wooden box lid that just needed a bit of sanding and a fresh coat of sealer to make it table-ready.

DOMESTIC HELP

Simplify buffet-style dinners with a little extra help in the dining room. Easily found wooden drawer organizers quickly convert into serviceable trays. Just add matching handles to the organizers and line them with fabric or wallpaper scraps ... a great way to coordinate your trays with your décor. Like the "distressed paint" look? See page 139 to copy the technique we used to age the white organizer.

Discover a *new* needlepoint of view

Shopping at the flea market yields many happy discoveries. Even handmade items like needlepoint pictures eventually find their way into resale markets. If you come across a piece of needlework that speaks to your heart, consider making it into a decorative pillow.

When your pillow features a true Renaissance man, only the best fabrics will do! Turn to page 143 to learn how easy it is to finish your needlework as a pillow with shirred welting.

Perennial favorites, Blue Boy and Pinkie model their needlepoint finery on ruffled throw pillows (page 143). And would you believe the framed portrait of Blue Boy is a paint-by-numbers flea market find?

Fabulous FIND

All things Americana are very collectible these days. This needlepoint featuring Old Glory and a Bald Eagle unites with brushed denim to make a stately box cushion (page 143).

Fabulous FIND

Soften the look of a new towel with a border of little granny squares and interesting buttons.

I t's hip to be square. And that makes these crocheted granny squares a valuable flea market find. The multi-colored blocks were originally whipstitched together, perhaps forming a table runner or doll afghan. But on their own, the little squares make retro embellishments for any number of household accessories. Granny would be so proud!

A stitch from time: individual squares tie a jar candle, photo album, and button box into a matched set.

Snappy
PHOTO DISPLAYS

When photography was new, "getting your picture made" was an elaborate production that yielded stuffy photos of somber subjects. The tradition of smiling for the camera probably didn't begin until the 1920's, when anyone could own and use inexpensive cameras like the Brownie. The slot in the side of this Argus® Seventy-five camera case (above) holds a wire photo tree, a nice way to display your own candid photos.

Are you smiling? These flea market cameras represent thirty-six years of snapshot history. Purchased frames are glued over the lens windows and inside the flash reflector. The new frames match the cameras after an application of black paint and a silver rub-on finish.

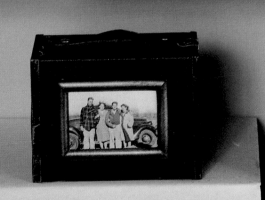

office
@HOME

Whether you need a little space for meeting work deadlines, writing letters, or just for paying bills, your home office should be uniquely you. In the next few pages, you'll see two completely different and totally wonderful ways to use flea market furnishings while creating your dream workspace.

The retro redo shown at left will help lighten any workload with its exotic colors, tropical print fabric, and the charm of a simpler era. Turn the page to learn how easy these makeovers can be!

AT THE
MILLER'S
8:00 PM

TROPIC *of* DISCUSSION

Every stress-free office should have a patio chair! Black paint refreshes the chair's finish while bark cloth renews the seat cushion. How-to's on page 142 make covering a round cushion almost effortless, and it's even easier to cover a lampshade with fabric. Just follow the directions on page 148.

Blackboard paint changes a framed print into a handy writing surface above the desk.

When work and play mingle this freely, any task seems easier to tackle! Black paint rejuvenates the sides, legs, and drawer fronts of this vintage desk. The drawer pulls and plastic inserts get the look of cast aluminum from a touch of silver paint. And surprise! — the refreshing key-lime color at the end of the desk is actually the side of the drawer, painted the happiest tropical shade we could find. See page 139 to recreate the faux agate desktop in shades of gray.

from *Perfume & Powder* TO PEN & PAPER

Now that you've discovered flea market style, your home office doesn't have to encompass an acre of faux wood grain or a mile of stainless steel. The secondhand items shown here work together under the inspiration of a floral-print fabric and some surprising decorator innovations. Turn the page for a closer look at this feminine workspace, then get started on creating your own stylish office. Lucky you!

A design for success: Purchase flea market furnishings for your home office and let your personality decide their final form. It's the easiest assignment you'll ever love.

OFFICE
Sweet

Decorate your home office with the same flourish you give your correspondence! Paint, fabric, and wooden appliqués blend mismatched flea market furnishings into a dainty — but functional — office suite. This glass-topped desk and the ribbon-lattice message board were originally parts of a vanity table. We share the easy instructions and painting technique on page 140.

Wooden appliqués beautify an in-box and recycling bin with glue-and-paint simplicity.

Left: Pour on the charm! A pitcher lamp (page 140) floods the desktop with light, while a vase acts as a graceful pencil cup. Frilly lace, a satin bow, and a piece of flea market jewelry sweeten the lampshade. Like all the decorator treasures in this ladylike office, the Victorian-style letter holder is a handy resale find.

Bottom, left: Every desk should have a clutter-catcher, especially one as dainty as this. New paint gives the molded resin dish a delicate look. The top of the desk is prettied up with some of the same vintage fabric that covers the chair seat.

TABLES
& CHAIRS

There's no reason to settle for bland, cookie-cutter furniture while uniqueness abounds in resale shops. Bringing such originality into your home and making it completely yours is much easier than you might think. On the next several pages, you'll find tables and chairs with brand-new attitudes … and styles that are refreshingly flea market.

farmhouse
memories

A little sanding along the edges gives this vanilla-toned dining set a timeworn look. Painter's tape makes it easy to paint stripes on the chairbacks and drop-leaf table.

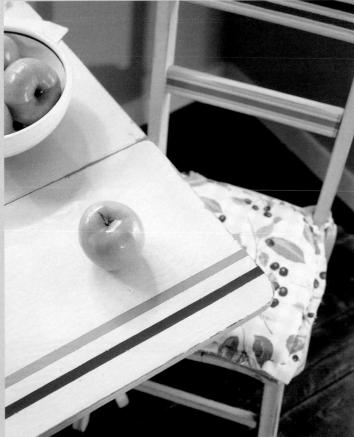

Color is key when uniting flea market furnishings. Crocheted doll-dress potholders, glued to plates, pick up the cheery hues of dish towels in retro prints. The reproduction towels hang from a café curtain rod and accent a pair of seat cushions. Covering the cushions is quick when you handsew with embroidery floss — just stitch around the cushion and trim with pinking shears. Ties of grosgrain ribbon hold each cushion in place.

HEAVEN SEEMS A LITTLE
CLOSER IN A HOUSE BESIDE
THE WATER

FISH STORY

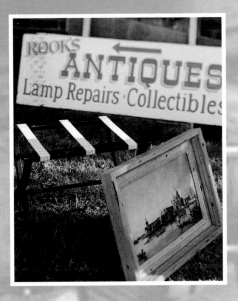

Giving in to the lure of a flea market luggage rack and a cast-off framed print yields a shadowbox table that showcases a fisherman's prized collection ...

Collectors will love our inventive table, and it can be made in no time using easy-to-find resale items! Transform a deep picture frame into a display tabletop by rubbing the frame with stain. Turn the picture over inside the frame, then cover the picture with split bamboo matting using spray adhesive. Cut a piece of glass to cover the frame, creating a shadowbox. Spiff up the luggage rack base with a coat of paint. We filled our table with fishing accessories to make a handsome end table, but the best part of this fun project is that you can fill the top with your own treasured collectibles.

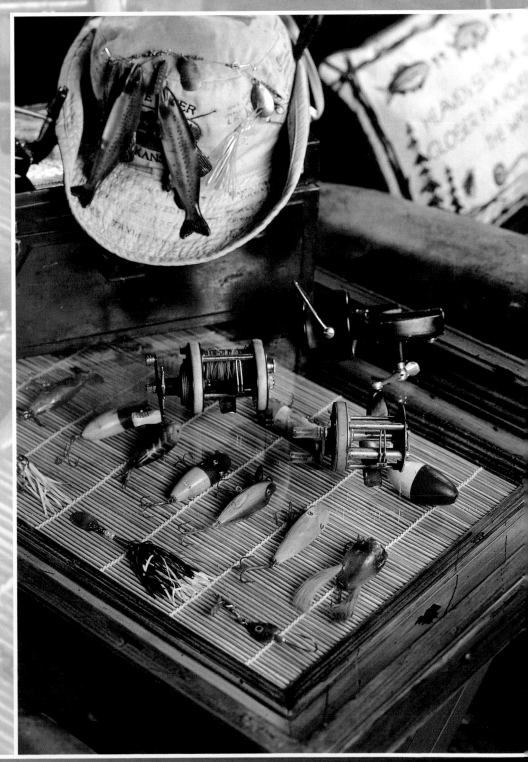

Flea market shoppers are always looking for the unusual, even if it's just a new way to use ordinary things. And if a secondhand treasure yields a bonus like extra storage, it's a bargain not to be missed. Easy redesigns like these unique tables complement a casual décor while providing space for more collectibles.

casual WITH CACHET

Opposite: This cedar chest rises up on fence post finials to catch coffee cups and conversation pieces. The polished-edge glass top protects a shining surface of copper leaf, the results of a fun-and-easy craft technique (page 140).

Above and right: A tea-tray style table plays host to a bottle collection. The look of aged red lacquer is easy to reproduce, using bold terra-cotta paint and aged oak gel stain. No need to refinish the top and shelf — line with wallpaper for an instant redo.

A MOVABLE FEAST
LIFE IS A PICNIC WHEN YOU'RE LIVING IN FLEA MARKET STYLE.

A simple paint technique (page 141) rejuvenates the top of this vintage card table and the backs of the folding chairs with the look of burled wood.

The good life … it's only a picnic away. Invite the best of your memories along by packing your car with familiar flea market finds: a cooler, a basket, a thermos, and a wooden folding table and chairs. The next time you feel the need to slow down and savor your day, you can make a getaway to the park … and to the good life.

TRUE COLORS

The role of tables in home décor is usually more functional than decorative, even when their task is to hold an eye-catching centerpiece or elevate a unique lamp. But your flea market table can be as much a focal point as any decorator accent, just by adding color to some or all of its surfaces. Let this trio of bright ideas give you a leg up on the possibilities.

Above and top right: This "mosaic" tabletop isn't tile and it isn't paint — it's paper napkins, cut apart and decoupaged in place. However, the table does wear new paint beneath the artful application. Learn this easy technique on page 141.

Opposite: Freedom of expression is a beautiful thing. Turn to page 141 to read about using painter's tape and star-shaped stickers, then let your pride show on your own glorious tabletop!

Left: The dainty table beneath the window wears pretty pinstripes on its top. Painter's tape keeps each line tidy while consecutive paint colors are applied.

LADDERBACK
SUCCESS STORIES

Start with a fabulous ladderback ...

... and give it a style that's right for you. It's the simplicity of design that makes this chair a prime canvas for the brushstrokes of decorator genius. Find your favorite perch here, or turn the page for more...

Chair of an American Heritage

It's a star-spangled glory! Paint the seat red and the chairback slats white. Apply star stickers when the slats are dry and repaint blue; peel off the stickers after drying. A striped cushion puts the finishing touch on this all-American chair.

All there, in black & white

"My Fair Chair" is no longer commonplace. Hepburn-esque bows and a frilly cushion set a scene that's sure to please Milady. Wouldn't it be lovely ... in *your* house? The change begins on page 144. Extraordinary!

A *rose* bouquet for you to chair

At the flea market, choose a trio of handkerchiefs. Hand stitch one to a purchased pillow for a seat cushion, and use the others to make a chairback cover for a freshly painted chair (page 143). Sweet and easy!

OUR INITIAL THINKING ON FLEA MARKET CHAIRS

Maybe it's a "chaircase"...
or perhaps it's just our way
of saying you only have
to take a few easy steps
to make your mark on
secondhand chairs.

$\mathcal{D}$ecorating with flea market style means exploring new ideas based on old concepts. Take a seat, for instance. You can choose an ordinary secondhand chair, dust it off, and be pleased with your purchase — or you can pull that chair up to your level of artistic comfort. We provide two sets of alphabets on pages 154 and 155 so you can add your special character to the chair of your choice.

Above: A regal armchair (page 144) sports a bold monogram in a gilded frame, proof that one should never apologize for leaning on formalities.

Below: Lucky is the lady whose repose is sweetened by this feminine chair (page 144).

An iron-on appliqué (glued, not pressed), buttons, and a thick coat of resin make sitting pretty ... pretty simple. Details on page 145.

COLLECT·

TABLES

No swan song for this unusual table — revived with paint and wallpaper, it became a collector's favorite display.

A re you looking for something to take your collection to the next level? Well, now you've found it!

With sturdy bases and safety ledges, tiered flea market tables like these are perfect for displaying fragile treasures.

What better way to
show off pieces of
chintzware than on a
delicate-looking table with
painted "pie crust" edges?

TIME TABLE

A little time is all it takes to update an old metal tray table. For instance, you can photocopy the rose print on page 157 to découpage onto a freshly painted tabletop. Add clock works and numerals and you'll have a dual-purpose table that looks as fresh as anything you'll find in retail shops. Turn to page 145 for more about this up-to-the-minute style!

Farm-fresh
FACES

Turn back the hands of time with flea market finds. It's amazing how many fresh looks for home décor can be found among jumbles of old things. Clock kits (page 145) can convert castoff items into working timepieces in just minutes, leaving you with time on your hands … and on your walls, and shelves, and countertops …

Left: This "pasture-ized" dairy clock is based on a wooden cheese box lid. The découpaged scene is a page from a flea market calendar. Photocopies of milk bottle seals mark the hours.

Above: A cardboard cheese box lid printed with a fetching milkmaid makes a refreshing clock base. Just sponge-paint the sides and add a clock kit.

Right: Put a lid on time — remove the knob from an old enamelware pot lid and insert a clock kit in the hole. Voilà! Instant clock.

ime marches on, leaving us with an abundant supply of artifacts from a century gone by. Using those leftover items to record the passage of time seems like the right thing to do, especially when the one-of-a-kind clocks you create look as good as these.

*O*TIME

Old frames are among the items that run the gamut from rustic to regal, and that means countless new timekeeping options for your flea market décor.

Leading a double life can be a good thing — a framed cardboard print does just that after its conversion to a clock/chalkboard. Spend just a little time reading the instructions on page 146, then photocopy the design on page 156 to make a noteworthy message center of your own.

AND A SEASON

Take it "easel." An old print puts a pleasant face on this easel-style flea market frame. The simple how-to's on page 146 are among the best timesaving advice available.

Imagine it: You're shopping at your favorite flea market when a shimmer of light catches your eye. You find a heap of shining earrings, bracelets, brooches, and necklaces … adornments discarded years ago when fashions changed. You smile and gather up these glittering treasures, glad you've discovered what the original owners never knew — old jewelry makes stunning home accents!

YOUR *Treasured* H·O·M·E

On a jewel-bedecked tabletop, earrings bloom in the centers of silk flowers. Beaded bracelets and necklaces wrap themselves around pillar candles or spill their bounty into a bowl. Strands of beads hold back the curtains, helping to frame a favorite view with old-fashioned finery. And all of it was done in an instant.

N A P K I N ❖ J E W E L R Y

Treat dinner guests to a taste of yesteryear — dress your dinner napkins in vintage costume jewelry! Looped around the first napkin (above, left) is a beaded choker with a narrow ribbon tied to each end. The free ends of the ribbon are threaded through the shank of a rhinestone button, then tied into a bow. The tasseled beauty (above, center) features an earring and a purchased tassel glued to a short length of wire-edged ribbon. The ribbon ends are glued together to form a ring. To make the starburst napkin ring (above, right), clasp a sparkling brooch over a length of wide satin ribbon, then knot the ribbon ends together around the napkin.

Want to add an element of fun to your dinner table? Make each place setting unique by using different patterns of china, glassware, and silverware. The diversity will be great food for conversation!

Like fabulous jewels, your evening
meals deserve elegant settings. Pearls were all
the rage when this china plate was manufactured
in the 1950's. The coiled bracelet of faux pearls with an
added bead dangle fits the era — and the napkin — in an instant!

In the 1950's, almost every young miss owned a jingly bracelet brimming with keepsake charms. We used the tiny trinkets from one to fashion a set of goblet tags. Besides being ornamental, the baubles are elegant solutions to the mix-ups that can occur when friends gather for conversation and refreshments.

For each goblet tag you want to make, just thread a single charm and the beads from an old necklace onto a short length of coiled memory wire, then crimp or loop the wire ends. You'll find memory wire in the jewelry-making supplies at your local craft store.

beauty,
charm
&

grace

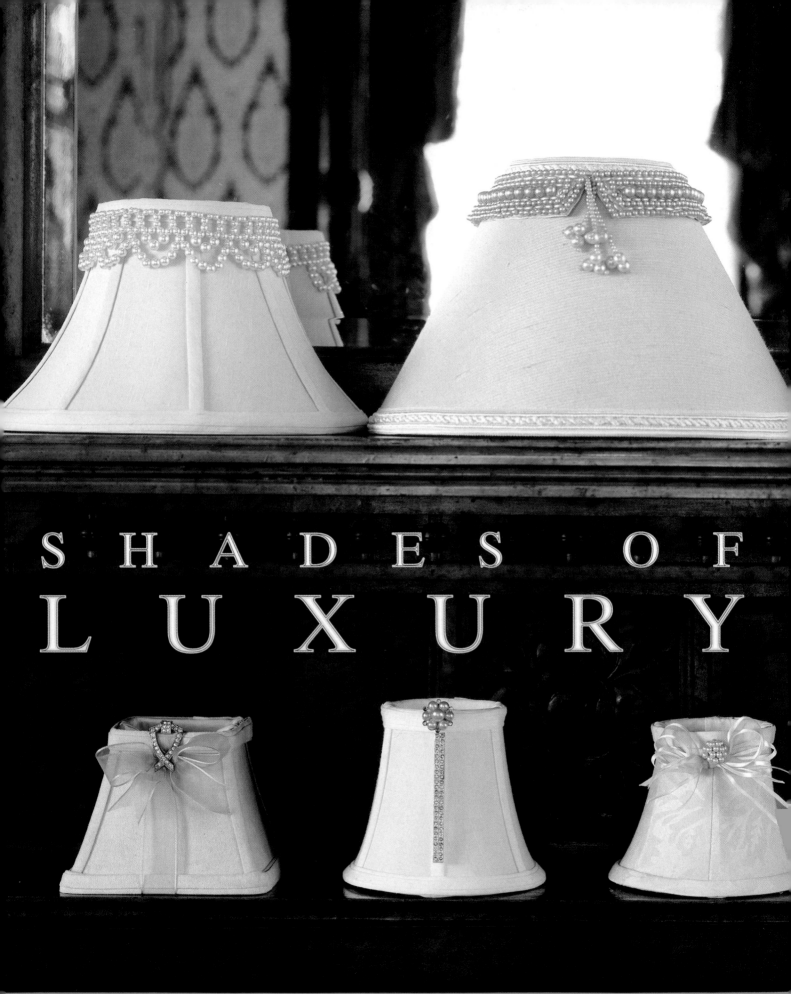

SHADES OF LUXURY

Pearls *OF* *wisdom*

For luxurious lighting in an instant, use flea market jewelry to adorn lampshades. Just a dot of glue or a quick stitch with needle and thread is all it takes to secure yesteryear's finery to the shade of your choice. Old brooches and pins are even easier to use — just stick them into the fabric of the shade.

The lovely curves of beaded sweater collars fit two of our lampshades (above, left and center) to perfection. Adding elegance to a trumpet shade (above, right) are a single-strand necklace, a flower pin, and a sheer ribbon bow.

Four little lampshades (below, left to right) receive classic elegance when enriched by tag sale jewelry: a shoe clip and ribbon bow, a rhinestone pin and screw-on earring, a pearl cluster earring with multi-loop bow, and a pearl drop pendant on satin ribbon.

S W E E T
Romance

Reward yourself with the sweeter things in life. Vintage beaded necklaces and flea market sugar bowls combine to create romantic hanging candleholders — in an instant! See page 146 for the easy directions.

One lump or two? Although the Fostoria Glass Company created this clear "cubist" sugar bowl in the early 20th century, a similar pattern was also produced by the Jeanette Company in both clear and colored glass.

Left: The lacy glass pattern called "Sandwich" is a familiar sight to resale shoppers. This diamond-shaped Sandwich sugar dish from Indiana Glass has helped satisfy sweet tooths since the 1920's.

Below: The shape of this MacBeth-Evans sugar bowl may be simple, but its "Stippled Rose Band" gives it plenty of personality. A closer look reveals traces of gold on the rim of the dish.

Right: What's in a name? In 1913, the Imperial Glass Company chose to call this delicate pattern simply "Frosted Block." With its loving-cup shape, this little dish is still just as sweet.

Above: This impressive beauty sports sturdy feet, angled handles, and eight gleaming sides. It has no identifying mark or etching but may be a glass "blank" from the A.H. Heisey Company.

Pillow JEWELRY

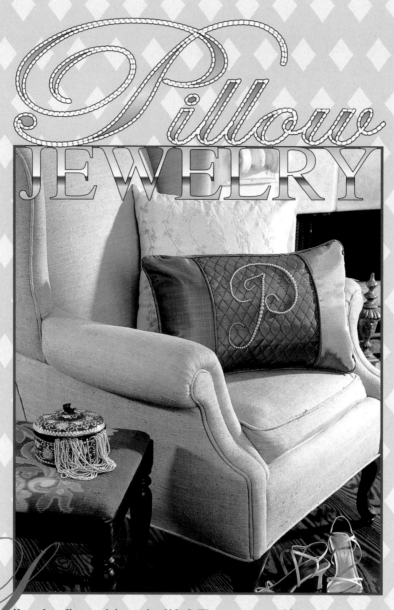

Like the finer things in life? Treat yourself to the riches of bejeweled pillows. Embellish purchased cushions with glittering necklaces, brooches, earrings, bracelets — whatever flea market bauble catches your eye. Go elegant with clear rhinestones and faux pearls or make your décor dazzling with a rainbow of colored jewels.

Thread a needle and use it to tack strings of pearls onto a satin pillow, shaping the necklaces into a stylish monogram. Remove the backs from clip-on earrings and glue them to the buttons of a purchased pillow. Or wrap a slender cushion with a necklace and add a clip-on earring.

TOP

Brass

Transform an old brass bowl with acrylic paint and easy "special effects." Cover all surfaces of the bowl with spray-on black primer, followed by black semi-flat paint. Brush the outside of the bowl with crackle medium, avoiding any decorative edges. Sponge barn red paint over the crackled surface and allow it to dry, then rub fine steel wool over the top edge of the bowl to expose a gleam of brass. For extra shine, sponge random highlights of metallic gold rub-on finish over the bowl's exterior. Like what you see? More classy brass makeover ideas are available at the turn of a page ...

Rediscover yesterday's brass accessories at your local flea market — you'll love how they go from tarnished to terrific with the greatest of ease.

To restore the good looks of this brass flea market lamp, we applied paint over the column using a quick marbling technique (page 146). The weighty base below the lamp's column also needed renewing. Thanks to paint and a metallic rub-on finish, it now imitates onyx with a shimmer of gold leaf. Perfection of form ... color enhanced!

AGED TO Perfection

These mismatched candlesticks had lost their luster but regained their appeal through an easy paint treatment. We sprayed the candlesticks with a red oxide primer, then painted them with light ivory acrylic paint. Gel wood stain was applied and wiped off with a soft towel. A light sanding allowed the red primer to show through, while an application of matte sealer protected our handsome handiwork. The entire process was completed in a flash, leaving lots of leisure time to enjoy the mellow beauty of our "Old World" collection.

While it's **true** that you can't improve on a **classic** form, even the most **pleasing** shapes can benefit from a bit of **artful** "aging."

WINNING METALS

With modern paint techniques, tarnished brass castoffs can take on a whole new life as decorator accents for your home. Remember to look beyond the tarnish and choose pieces with interesting shapes and details that will be enhanced by their makeovers. Instructions for these planters are on page 147.

If the boldness of brass doesn't fit your décor, try updating secondhand accessories with feminine fabric and a touch of painted panache. These old candle sconces only needed a little encouragement to shine anew — without candles or electrical wiring! Battery-operated candlestick lamps allow these petite lights to be placed on any wall. See the instructions on the facing page for the sweet-and-easy details.

sweetness & light

Brighten your outlook with a tasteful renovation that's pretty as a picture. A metal candle sconce flaunts a new finish with paint, fabric, and a refurbished frame. Turn to page 148 for the how-to's.

These delicate light fixtures will lend romantic appeal to a powder room or bedroom — and no one will ever guess they were once tarnished brass sconces! Simply spray the sconces with primer, then paint them white. To add some age, brush on a light oak stain, and rub it off with a soft towel. Adhere medallions of fabric to the wall plates. Insert a battery-operated candlestick into each sconce. Tie pink-and-white striped ribbon around the candle cups. Glue pink satin ribbon around the bottoms of the lampshades, then glue open-weave trim over the ribbon and attach the shades to the lamps.

Modern alchemy transformed the tarnished brass surfaces on this glass lamp, giving it the look of aged silver. And although we can't tell you how to change lead into precious metals, these four easy steps will show you how to impart your own fashionable finish to any metal — no magic needed!

M E T A L

1 Don't pass up a flea market lamp because the metal finish has seen brighter days! Many older lamps have metal accents that, with a little tender-loving care, can be brought back to life with a new shine and sparkle. To get started, you will need a soft cloth, Rub 'n Buff® metallic finish, black gel stain or acrylic paint, rubber gloves, and a paintbrush.

2 Prepare lamp surfaces with a household cleaner to remove dust and dirt. With a soft cloth, apply Rub 'n Buff to tarnished metal areas, let dry, and buff to remove excess finish.

3 Use a gel stain or make your own by mixing one-part water with one-part black acrylic paint. Brush the stain onto the metal — immediately wipe the area with a soft cloth to remove the excess (allow some of the stain to remain in the cracks and crevices to add instant age).

4 Our bargain lamp looks new again. Rub 'n Buff comes in gold, bronze, and silver metallic finishes so you can choose the look you want. You can even apply Rub 'n Buff to the lamp cord!

morphosis

ILLUMINATIONS

Want a big reward for just a little effort? Invest in flea market lamps! Available at bargain prices, they offer function as well as endless decorating options. On the next few pages, you'll find our latest collection of enlightened ideas — old lamps made new again with easy updates, such as quick applications of paint or stain on the bases, or revamped lampshades (see how on page 148). You'll also discover lamps made using secondhand collectibles … true one-of-a-kinds that are sure to spark new ideas for additions to your décor!

Above: New fabric, ribbon, and braid return the oval shade on this candelabra-style lamp to its original elegance. The lamp base wears a fresh coat of green paint on its wooden section and a corded tassel for a soft touch of style. And for the grand finale — a grand finial! An antique glass door knob sparkles in its exciting new role.

Opposite: Guests might mistake this hospitable lamp for a recent retail purchase, but it's a resale beauty topped by a new lampshade covered in creamy yellow fabric. The brass areas are brightened with a rub-on metallic finish, while a corded tassel about the base complements the trim on the shade.

Very "Lady-light"

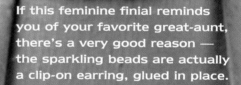

If this feminine finial reminds you of your favorite great-aunt, there's a very good reason — the sparkling beads are actually a clip-on earring, glued in place.

Left: To recreate this well-heeled lamp, insert two plastic foam balls into an antique shoe. Hot glue a candlestick lamp to the top ball. Use short lengths of wire to insert silk flowers and a bow into the foam. Cover a lampshade with feminine fabric and glue lace around its edge.

Below: See page 149 to easily recreate vintage style using a flea market swing-arm lamp, wallpaper, and paint.

Opposite: This pocketbook lamp is a snap to put together! We cut an opening in the back of the slim purse to allow room for the lamp base. After placing the lamp and a pair of white gloves in the purse, we wired the purse clasp to the lamp, then added a ribbon bow to the handle. The lampshade is fashionably finished with upholsterer's gimp and fabulous fake fur trim.

The original owners of this 1950's purse and the elegant Victorian boot probably never dreamed that their accessories would become highlights of 21st century décor. And they would surely have been surprised to see the look of circa 1900 tin ceiling panels copied onto an easy-to-make desk lamp. However, we think women of all eras would agree, the results are completely charming and very "lady-light."

Even without their stoppers, crystal decanters can offer refreshing style. Bottle-adapter lamp kits, sprayed with chrome paint, give these decanters a second life. And plain lampshades go posh when covered in fabric and edged with tasseled or beaded fringe. Bias-cut fabric strips or gimp cover the lampshade rims. Supporting the silver-and-light theme are a cut glass luncheon plate and a silver-plated tray.

silver and light

Searching for a wise investment? Silver is a sure thing, especially when you buy it at flea market prices. For exciting dividends, top off your silver and crystal selections with lamp kits. Turn to page 150 to see the variety of kits available.

When you're shopping for silver wares, don't pass up tarnished accessories. A little patina can be a very good thing. In fact, over-polishing may actually reduce the perceived value of an older silver piece. Instead of spending time cleaning every little smudge, enjoy your silver … just as it is!

Candle power gets a boost: This silver candlestick (above, left) is a flea market prize. Chrome paint matches a bottle-adapter lamp kit to the candlestick, while beaded trim and silk flowers add old-fashioned loveliness to the shade.

A screw-on lamp kit spotlights a silver bookend (above). The lampshade glows with new fabric and beaded ribbon trim.

light up his LIFE

Decorating for the man in your life just got easier! Memorabilia and collectibles with masculine appeal abound at flea markets. Just add a little imagination to your purchase and you'll be ready to augment a lamp with anything from model airplanes to baseball mitts. The lamps shown here will be extra-pleasing for the recipient — you won't have to borrow tools from his workbench to create them!

A candlestick lamp shines on this stack of collectibles. Tacky wax secures each piece without damaging its finish. Or try hot glue on your tin — it's easy to loosen with the heat of a blow dryer.

Through the years, beverage manufacturers have created special-edition decanters in a variety of shapes, including cars, landmarks, and even famous persons. A display lamp kit is an excellent way to show off a prize collectible like this duck decanter. Just stain or paint the wooden base that's included in the kit, assemble the lamp fixture, then add a lampshade and the decanter of your choice.

dappled designs

Although the glaze on this 19th century spongeware pitcher has a few tiny cracks called "crazing," there are no serious flaws in the piece that would prevent the use of the prized antique as a vase.

Bold in its simplicity, spongeware is enjoying a resurgence of popularity not seen since the 19th century. Because most American housewives of that era could not afford the Chinese porcelain that was so fashionable then, the introduction of spongeware made it possible for them to enjoy the same blue pigment on sturdy pottery. You can easily copy this historic look for your modern home by sponging acrylic paint onto purchased lampshades. For the lamps to go under your newly dappled shades, experiment with secondhand kitchen items — you'll be pleased with the tasteful results. Turn to page 149 to see how we converted the petite pitcher and the collectible glass coffee jar into useful little lamps.

MILK GLASS
HAS SCENE THE LIGHT

Say **merci** *to the French for the textile known as "toile." The smooth fabric printed with pastoral images is popular once again. To fashion these petite lamps, we've paired some samplings of toile with a classic American favorite — milk glass.*

Above: Hot glue holds a candlestick lamp inside a milk glass compote, and moss covers the lamp base. The mini lampshade is covered with toile and trimmed with ribbon. Creating a ruffle with wire-edged ribbon is easy. Folding back and crimping a half-inch of wire at one end, push the ribbon along the wire on one edge to gather it; trim and crimp end of wire.

Opposite: Boudoir lamps gain height when tucked into milk glass urns. Button-centered ribbon bows line up on four-sided lampshades.

Above: A jaunty blue ribbon weaves through the open spaces in the rim of a candy dish. The candlestick lamp is secured by hot gluing it to a plastic foam ball that fits snugly inside the dish. Moss and a sprig of flowers cover the ball.

Below: It just doesn't get any sweeter than this: with a little hot glue, a milk glass sugar bowl becomes a base for its own candlestick lamp. Silk flowers ring the top edge of the toile-covered shade, while ribbon adds a flourish to the shade and weaves through the edges of a square glass tray.

Romance
OF
CANDLES

Candlelight … it's always been a favorite companion.
For special events or quiet evenings at home, it
spreads a soft glow from votive cups, candelabras,
candlesticks, and chandeliers. But did you know there
are many more ways to enjoy this gentle radiance?
Let the ideas on the following pages inspire you to
combine the romance of candles with other familiar
yet unexpected items … from the past, from your
heart, and from the flea market!

One of the benefits of flea market shopping is the license for creativity — when you pay less than retail for wonderful things, you feel free to use your purchases in unique ways. Glassware is a shining example of how an old form can sparkle in a new function.

Right: The hollow pedestal of an overturned cake stand becomes a charming little vase. Circling the pedestal are rose-scented candles in matching votive cups.

Opposite: Orphaned stemware is an easy-to-find and usually inexpensive resale item. On this large platter, inverted goblets of varying heights support a mingling of votive cups with coordinating candles. Cheers!

ulterior VOTIVES

candleholder ideas that MAKE THE CUT

Glassware is always a strong contender for teaming with candles. Your prospects of locating a promising vase, bowl, or bottle at your local flea market are excellent. Remember, it doesn't matter whether you choose cut crystal or pressed glass — either will give a sparkling performance in the candlelight.

Floating candles are set adrift in this water-filled glass bowl (above), while a decorative base, borrowed from another secondhand treasure, heightens interest.

The unique glass-and-metal candlesticks (above) are clever conversions. We just removed the wiring and sockets from a pair of boudoir lamps that no longer functioned. Chubby tapers fit perfectly into the resulting bases, while bow-tied velvet ribbons ready this dapper duo for every occasion.

Vinegar cruets that have lost their stoppers make classy little candleholders. They are usually inexpensive and plentiful at resale shops. A mirrored tray reflects the loveliness of gleaming glass, beautiful bows, and faux flowers.

Burning calories: For a healthier glow, toss out the candy in favor of candlelight! Castoff candy dishes make radiant candleholders, especially when filled with candle gel. Ribbon and silk flowers help sweeten the mix. Never worked with candle gel before? It's an easy-to-use candlemaking supply you can find at your local hobby store.

In addition to their beauty, gel candles generally last much longer than standard wax candles! Although the supplies to make gel candles are available in kit form, you can custom-fit your candles to your containers by purchasing clear gel, colors, fragrance, and wicks separately. Carefully follow the manufacturers' instructions and precautions. These should also include tips to guide you in creating special effects, such as the "fizzy" appearance of trapped air bubbles. The rewards of your easy endeavors will be sweet, indeed!

CLEARLY UNIQUELY CANDLEHOLDERS

Here's a butter idea: Reassign your collection of flea market butter dishes to "lighter" duties — as candleholders! A ball candle is a perfect fit for the curve of an old-fashioned, domed keeper. Or place wicks in the lid of an oblong butter dish, add melted candle gel, and use the base of the dish as a cover.

"PARDON ME...MAY I HAVE

No smoking, please — we can't spare the ashtrays! A spark of inspiration teams these resale treasures with candles and old costume jewelry. The wax pillars (opposite, from left) get their glitz from sheer ribbon and a clip-on earring, a beaded necklace wired in place with a silk flower, and a circle brooch threaded on ribbon. The votive/ashtray trio (left) wear identical snippets from a beaded necklace and bows of satin-edged ribbon. Snugged together for a perfect fit (below), two square candles look cozy in a rectangular ashtray. The sheer ribbon tied around the pair is threaded with pearly beads from a bracelet.

A LIGHT?"

A Light Aloft

Let flea market style elevate your expectations of what romantic lighting should be — and where it should be! This outdoor "candle-lier" is an electric light fixture with its wiring removed. You can use a shepherd's crook to hang the candle-lier anywhere in the garden or yard. We give the easy instructions for this lovely light transformation on page 151.

ocking gently in the breeze, this metal and glass light fixture cover brightens a garden path. On page 151, we tell how you can perform the same outdoor magic with paint, wire, and flea market jewelry. So enlightening!

Opposite, below: Swirling water in a hot tub invites the romance of candlelight. This scallop-edged dish holding a candle cup is actually a cut glass globe from an electric light fixture. Turn to page 151 to trade incandescence for romance.

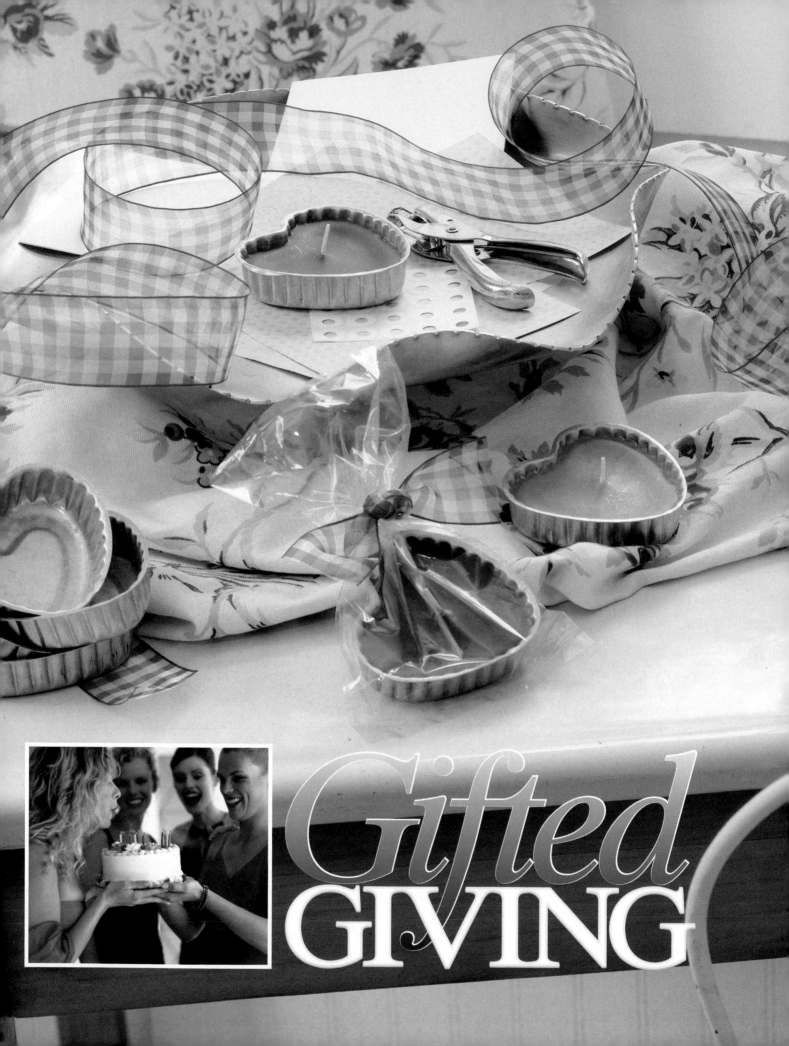

Gifted GIVING

Resale items are the clever basis for all the gift
ideas you'll find in these next few pages. So keep an eye
out for "giftables" nestled among yesteryear's treasures.
The sweetheart candles shown here are easy — just add wicks
and melted wax to flea market molds; attach handcrafted
tags made from cardstock and decorative paper.

gifts of good scents

Sweet in so many ways, handkerchief sachets are also simple to create! Bundle your favorite potpourri in a muslin square, then wrap it in a vintage hankie and tie with coordinating ribbons. Insert the stem of a silk blossom between the gathers.

Share a cup of cheer with someone special. An orphaned punch cup is an ideal vessel for a gel candle. Place an anchored wick inside the cup and add melted gel. Choose a gift box and ribbon in colors to coordinate with the candle, top with a silk flower, and you'll be serving up a beautiful presentation!

THE *joy* OF BASKETS ...

Skip the boredom
of wrapping a box —
present your offerings
in a basket! Elegant gift-giving
ideas like these await you in
flea markets everywhere.

BASKETS OF *joy*

Remember the gift table at the last birthday party or shower you attended? Was the most memorable gift a basket, filled with thoughtful items? Rather than wrap your gifts, you can bestow baskets of joy, easily and inexpensively. A fresh coat of paint with a simple "whitewash" finish, page 151, took these gift-laden beauties from resale to remarkable in just minutes. For an extra-special touch, use vintage napkins or doilies as basket liners.

essence OF GIVING

The thoughtfulness of flowers in flea market containers can be a gift in itself. Spice bottles make versatile vases, and they're just the right size to hold short-stemmed blossoms. Tie ribbons around a number of spice bottles and arrange them in a glass dish as shown on this page. Or, for a larger centerpiece, arrange the bottle vases on a cakestand like the candles on page 98.

Just as red roses are linked with love, these little spice bottles are linked with lovely ribbon. Entwine and knot two lengths of ribbon between each bottle and tie into bows at the ends.

Purple paint renews a flea market spice caddy. Its four matching bottles can be used as individual vases or kept together with the caddy for a combined bouquet.

Cookin' up heartwarming gifts...

Thinking about gifting someone with your homemade pickles or a favorite store-bought treat? If you prepare ahead, you won't have to worry about containers for your food gifts. All it takes is an assortment of flea market jars with lids, and vintage linens with printed designs. Make color photocopies of the linens, cut the designs from the paper, and glue them to your jars. For a small jar, you could even gather a photocopy of an entire napkin or handkerchief around its lid and tie it with a bow.

Crunchy snack mix will be
welcomed by new neighbors.
This collectible jar has its own
happy design, so the gift tag
needn't be fancy.

Flea market wares make tasteful gifts. An old metal basket can hold a jar of dry ingredients for soup, a roll of cheery napkins, and perhaps an enamelware soup mug. Who wouldn't love getting such a thoughtful gift? When creating gift tags, a color copier makes it easy for you to enlarge or reduce the designs you find on vintage linens. Clip your designs from the copy paper, paste them onto card stock, and add your greeting.

...from your kitchen

The zinc lid of this old gallon jar has a wire bale, making it easy to deliver a zesty gift of ice-cold lemonade. And a vintage freezer jar presents a zippy treat of homemade pickles.

GARDENER'S GIFTS

Surprise a gardener with a selection of gifts from the flea market. Plant flowers in unexpected containers. Provide a caddy to keep necessities within easy reach. Think of little ways to bring the beauty of the garden indoors and consider small items that might lend household convenience to the garden. Look around the flea market to see how many gift ideas take root within your imagination.

Right: A flat of berry baskets filled with cheerful flowers conveys wishes for sunnier days ahead.

Little blossoms have big impact when presented in enamelware mugs. The handy tray can carry cool drinks outdoors to a thirsty gardener. Copy the vintage-style gift tags on page 153.

To truly thrill a gardener's heart, give a gift that makes her beloved hobby easier! The freshly painted sections of this unique aluminum caddy hold gloves, row markers, hand tools, and packets of seed.

alfrescoSTYLE

Every bit as wonderful as it looks ...
it's summertime and the living is alfresco —
with flea market style, of course.

If you've found a sturdy wire container at your local flea market, you've found a prize! The dip-coated egg baskets and painted milk crate shown here were originally employed by farmers and dairy workers to transport their goods. Although the handy holders have been retired for decades, they've adapted very well to their new jobs as patio planters. Moss lines the baskets and covers the flowerpot, adding the softness of nature to the rugged look of coated metal wire.

down to the
WIRE

friendly TABLE TALK

Revive the neighborly days of back-porch visits by adding a touch of nostalgia to your outdoor décor. Fold-down steps on this old step stool make it an instant multi-level table. New paint freshens its look, while an overturned tray widens the top step. And the "bowl-me-over" table (opposite) couldn't be simpler to create. Look around your local resale shops with an eye for other quick conversions. You'll find plenty of items that will give your porch or patio a bit of friendly, flea market style.

A stack of enamelware bowls
makes a sturdy pedestal for a
tabletop of tempered glass.
Double-stick foam mounting
tape secures the bowls without
damaging their surfaces.

*A washtub on casters may not be high tech …
but the wheels of progress will never fade
our squeaky-clean memories of yesterday.*

RUB-A-DUB TUB

Left: Restore the stand of an old washtub with bright-white, rustproof paint. Then fill the tub with ice and summer treats.

It's the earliest of washing machines, minus two important working parts: a pair of chapped hands. Celebrate your freedom from the days of hand-scrubbed laundry by converting an old washtub into something fun!

Above and right: Create a cozy table-and-chairs combination by topping your washtub with a window sash. Overlay the sash with a sheet of glass for a smooth dining surface. Complete the set with white wooden chairs, accented with red paint-marker dots.

WE SEE
great
POSSIBILITIES...

Keeping cool while enjoying the great outdoors is the biggest challenge of summer. Through the years, manufacturers have risen to that challenge, continually providing coolers of every description to keep our picnics fresh and our beverages icy cold. So what's to be done with an old ice chest that leaks or has lost its lid? The way we see it, nothing says "warm weather fun" more clearly than a nostalgia-evoking aluminum cooler filled with fresh flowers. If there's a sunny-day get-together in your future, let someone else provide the lemonade … you'll be bringing the coolest centerpiece of summer!

canoe?

If there's room to open a basket, there's room to dine alfresco. And if you aren't paddling your canoe alone, it's nice to share fresh flowers with your rowing partner. A little flea market ice chest will keep the blossoms perky.

Stools Out For Summer

Need an instant table for a summer of front porch entertaining? Grab a pair of stools at the flea market. They don't need to be a matched pair, but they do need to be the same height. Paint them however you please, then glue an assortment of bottle caps and buttons to the seats. Position the stools under a piece of tempered glass with polished edges. At summer's end, you'll love your instant table even more—it's super-easy to store away until next year!

PLAYFUL PLANTERS

Round stickers and acrylic
paint (see page 151) spread
delightful dots over a "fun-nel"
nosegay cone and a cheerful
quartet of flowerpots (opposite).
Paint jazzes up the interior of the
old tool box, too.

A bleeding heart finds joy again! Its new cachepot is a flea-market coal scuttle with a fresh "lining" of fuschia acrylic paint.

Tired of topiaries? Irked by ivy? Maybe it's not the plant that's making you itch for something different — it could be the planter. Here's our fun cure for gardener's regret: Combine the most offbeat of secondhand containers with the most surprising of paint colors. Now you've got playful planters with presence *and* pizzazz. It's enough to make a weeping ficus smile.

COUNTRY
flower pots & pans & kettles & urns & tins & sifters & tc.

Are they pot stickers or pan handlers? Whatever you choose to call them, these fun flea market hybrids give new meaning to the term "kitchen garden." To grow your own, use a drill and a screwdriver to graft an old kitchen container to the end of a freshly painted spindle. Plant something green in the container, then stake the spindle in the ground. A bumper crop of smiles is guaranteed. 🫖

how to do it ...

Just follow these easy instructions & get the fuss-free, satisfying results you want!

Fabulous Finds
Page 9

Combed Cabinet

Paint the cabinet with a basecoat of yellow semi-gloss paint and allow to dry.

Mix brown paint and glazing medium, then brush the mixture over the basecoat — do not allow the mixture to dry until after combing. Drag a combing tool (see photo below) through the wet glaze mixture, picking up the glaze and allowing the basecoat to show through (create patterns by turning the comb different ways). Wipe the comb clean each time you lift it from the surface.

Painting combs are available in a wide variety of shapes and "tooth" patterns. Experiment with several!

Cut cardboard panels to fit the sides of the cabinet, then cover them with fabric. Hot glue the panels to the cabinet.

Little Kitchen Helpers
Page 19

Cookie Tin

Remove the lid of a decorative tin and mask off the handles. Spray the container with primer, then with several coats of white spray paint. (We left the lid of our tin its original color.)

Color copy a portion of a vintage floral tablecloth, then cut a piece of the copy to fit the lid. Copy the "Cookies" label, page 152. Apply a coat of clear sealer to both sides of the copies.

Use découpage glue to adhere the copies to the container and lid and as a sealer to protect the surfaces.

Tip: The same look can be achieved by using color photocopies on self-adhesive paper. No need for glue, simply cut out the labels and smooth in place.

Table Service
Page 21

Flatware Caddy

Paint a wooden flatware organizer using your favorite color. Rub a candle randomly over the basecoat. Paint the organizer white. Lightly sand the organizer, revealing the basecoat and some of the underlying wood.

Make coordinating organizer liners from strips of fabric-covered cardboard cut to fit in the bottom of each section. Attach a decorative metal handle to each end.

Office@Home
Page 31

Agate Faux Finish

Paint the desktop pale grey and allow to dry. Using dark grey and two lighter shades of grey paint, dip a dampened natural sponge piece into the paint, mixing the colors as you pick up the paint. Blot sponge on a paper towel to remove excess paint, then use a light stamping motion

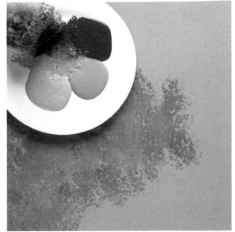

to paint over the basecoat, allowing some of the basecoat to show through. Allow paint to dry.

Randomly sponge dark grey paint over the surface and allow to dry.

Sponge on a final coat of light grey and allow to dry.

From Perfume & Powder ...
Pages 32–35

Country French Ladies Office

Enhance your office accessories with glued-on wooden appliqués, then paint all wooden areas white. Wash the decorative areas with a mixture of equal parts water and blue acrylic paint, letting the paint settle into the crevices. Use a soft cloth to wipe the washed areas, removing some of the paint.

Use undiluted blue acrylic paint to accent your chair with stripes, then cover the cushion with coordinating fabric.

The desk base is made from the pedestals of an old vanity, with fabric pieces cut to fit the tops. Add new hardware to the drawers and a large piece of glass with polished edges for the desktop.

For the message board, remove the mirror from the frame. Cut a piece of foam core board to fit the frame, then cover the board with batting and fabric. Use lengths of ribbon to make evenly spaced diamonds, gluing the ends to the back of the board. Wrap a length of thin ribbon around each ribbon intersection, then thread a button onto the ribbon, double-knotting ribbon at front.

To back the message board, cut a piece of mat board the same size as the message board and hot glue it to the back; hot glue the board inside the frame. Attach picture hanging wire to the frame; hang board with bottom edge resting on desktop.

To make the lamp, hot glue plastic foam into a pitcher for added height ... glue a candlestick lamp to the foam. Add foam around the lamp, then cover it with moss.

Casual with Cachet
Page 42

Metal-Leaf-Topped Coffee Table

Prepare the chest for metal leafing by cleaning the surface, then use painter's tape to mask around the section to be covered. Apply adhesive size, then press copper leaf sheets onto the surface at different angles to create a mottled effect. Apply sealer to the surface, and allow it to dry. Remove the painter's tape, and outline the copper-leafed area with self-adhesive copper foil tape. To add height, attach fence post finials to the bottom of the chest for legs. Before using as a table, top chest with a piece of glass with polished edges.

A Movable Feast
Page 45

Faux Finish Table and Chairs

Create the look of burled wood on a weathered wooden card table and chairs. Our table has a picturesque scene, which we chose to accentuate by painting only the table edges. Use painter's tape to mask along the edges of the center square to paint the border, then apply a coat of light brown paint. Dry brush the painted area with antique metallic gold paint.

Beginning with the light brown sections, mix an equal amount of light colored gel wood stain with clear acrylic glaze; brush the mixture over the surface. Press a small damp sponge into the wet mixture; twist and lift straight up, creating a circular pattern. Overlap circles and vary the amount of pressure on the sponge. Repeat to paint the dark brown sections with a mixture of dark gel stain and glaze. Allow the paint to cure.

For the decorative gold lines, place strips of tape ⅛" apart along the edges of the painted sections. Apply metallic gold wax between the strips of tape, allow to dry, then remove the tape. Seal the table and chairs with water-based polyurethane.

True Colors
Page 46

Flag Sofa Table

Paint the entire table white and allow it to dry. To create a field for the stars, tape off a section in the upper left corner with painter's tape. Arrange large star stickers within the taped border, making sure the edges adhere well so the top color does not bleed under them. Sponge paint the star field blue and allow it to dry overnight. Carefully remove the stickers and tape.

Using the front edge of the table as the first stripe, and spacing stripes evenly from front to back, tape off the flag's stripes and sponge paint them red. When dry, carefully remove the tape.

Page 47

Mosaic "Tiled" Table

Paint the bottom portion of your table, then the tabletop with coordinating paint colors (your tabletop color will become the "grout" between your paper napkin "tiles"). A light color of paint for the grout works best, as the appliquéd napkins will become translucent.

Cut the borders from cocktail napkins, then separate the plies. Using only the top ply and starting from the middle and working outward, position the napkin centers and border pieces on the tabletop, leaving a space between each piece. Using Aleene's® Paper Napkin Appliqué glue, adhere the napkin pieces to the tabletop. Apply several coats of glue over the entire tabletop to seal the surface.

MAKING A BASIC PILLOW

Whether you are converting a framed needlepoint piece into a pillow, making a box cushion, or a chair cover with a ruffle, these basic instructions apply to all the pillows:

1. Use a ½" seam allowance for all sewing unless otherwise indicated.

2. When sewing seams, match the right sides and raw edges.

3. Leave an opening along the bottom edge large enough for turning and inserting fiberfill or a pillow form.

4. After sewing fronts and backs together, turn right side out, carefully pushing corners outward. Insert pillow form, if used, then sew opening closed.

5. Refer to each pillow for specific details.

ADD A DECORATIVE EDGE

RUFFLE

1. Measure the pillow top circumference and multiply by 2½. Multiply desired finished ruffle width by 2 and add 1" (for example, for a 2" wide ruffle cut a 5" wide strip by the determined length); cut a piece of fabric (piecing if necessary) the determined measurements.

2. Matching right sides, sew short ends together; press the seam allowance open.

3. Matching wrong sides, fold the ruffle in half lengthwise and press. Gather ruffle along raw edges, distributing gathers evenly to fit around pillow top. Baste ruffle to right side of pillow top.

WELTING

Covered Welting

1. Measure the circumference of the pillow top and add 1". Cut a length of medium diameter cotton cording this length. Cut a bias strip of fabric (piecing if necessary) the same length as the cording and wide enough to wrap around cording plus 2".

2. Center cording on the wrong side of the bias strip; fold strip over cording. Use a zipper foot to machine baste along the length of the strip close to the cording. Trim the seam allowance.

Shirred Welting

1. Measure the circumference of the pillow top and add 1". Cut a length of thick cotton cording this length. Multiply this length by 2½. Loosely measure the circumference of cording and add 2". Cut a bias strip of fabric (piecing if necessary) the determined measurements.

3. Center cording on the wrong side of the bias strip; fold strip over cording. Use a zipper foot to machine baste along the length of the strip close to the cording for 10". Leave the needle in fabric and raise the presser foot. Hold cording while pushing the fabric strip behind the needle until it is gathered tightly. Continue stitching and gathering until cording is covered. Trim the seam allowance.

Attaching the Welting

1. Beginning at center bottom and matching raw edges, pin welting to the right side of the pillow top, clipping seam allowance as needed to turn corners.

2. Starting 1" from one end of the welting, baste welting to the right side of your pillow top, stopping 2" from other end. Cut welting so ends overlap by 1".

Fig. 1

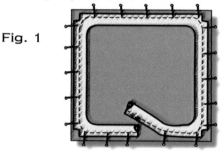

3. Remove 1" of basting from one end of welting. Holding fabric away from cord, trim cord ends to meet exactly. Turning one end of welting fabric under ½", insert one end of welting into the other; baste in place.

Fig. 2

Pages 22 – 23

Musketeer with Shirred Welting and Boy or Girl Pillows with Ruffles

Before cutting needlepoint canvas, draw a square or rectangle on the canvas the desired size for the pillow front. Stay stitch along marked lines, then cut just outside stitching.

For a pillow front with a fabric border, add the desired-size border to the top and bottom, then to each side of your pillow center. For pillow back, cut a piece from fabric the same size as your pillow front.

Follow "Add A Decorative Edge," if desired, to add a ruffle or welting.

Page 23

Eagle Box Pillow

For a pillow form, cut a piece of thick foam (ours measures 2¾" thick) 1" smaller than the pillow top.

For the pillow sides, measure the circumference and depth of the foam, then add 1" to each measurement. Cut a

strip of fabric the determined measurements, (piecing if necessary). With right sides together, stitch short ends of side strip together; press seam open.

Follow "Add A Decorative Edge" to make and attach the welting to the front and back pieces of the pillow cover.

Sew the side strip to the pillow front, then sew the remaining raw edge of the side strip to the pillow bottom.

Page 31

Round Chair Cushion

Measure the diameter of the chair seat, then cut a circle of foam for a pillow form. Add 1" to the measurement and cut two circles of fabric for the cushion top and bottom.

For the cushion sides, measure the circumference and depth of the pillow form, then add 1" to each measurement. Cut a strip of fabric the determined measurements, (piecing if necessary). With right sides together, stitch short ends of side strip together; press seam open.

Follow "Add A Decorative Edge" to make and attach the welting to the front

and back pieces of your cushion covering.

Sew the side strip to the cushion top, then sew the remaining raw edge of the side strip to the cushion bottom.

Page 51

Charming Seat Cover

Use kraft paper to make a pattern of the chair seat (drawing around uprights). Add a ½" seam allowance. Using pattern, cut one seat cover top and one bottom (mark position of each upright on the wrong side of the fabric pieces).

For welting and ruffle base length, measure from one upright, across the seat front, to the other upright.

To make welting, follow "Covered Welting."

To make ruffle, follow "Ruffle," Steps 1 and 3. For Step 2, hem short raw edges by turning each short edge under twice ¼" to the wrong side; press, then stitch in place.

Baste welting to the right side of the seat cover top from one upright mark to the other. Baste ruffle to right side of cover top over welting.

All There in Black & White
Page 50

Ladderback Luxury

Paint the chair white, then paint the desired sections of the rungs and spindles black.

Cut fabric strips from toile fabric and use découpage glue to adhere the strips to sections of the rungs and spindles ... when dry, apply another coat or two of glue over the fabric to seal it.

To accent the chairback, drill two holes about three inches apart in each slat. Thread ribbon through the holes, tying the ribbon into bows at the front.

Rose Bouquet Chair
Page 51

Chairback Slip

This simple chairback cover is made by sewing three buttons through the top

edges of two same-sized handkerchiefs ... simply drape it over the chairback.

Our Initial Thinking ...
Page 53

Cream Monogram Chair

Begin by painting a wooden chair with cream acrylic paint.

Find a picture frame to fit the chairback. Sizing to fit in your frame, make a photocopy of a letter from the alphabet on page 155 ... paint the letter with acrylic paint, then outline it with a permanent marker.

Cut a cardboard backing to fit into the frame. Adhere the monogram to the backing with découpage glue, then seal the surface with the glue. Hot glue the monogram in the frame. Apply double-faced foam mounting tape to the back of the frame and press into place on the center of the chairback.

Recover the chair seat with coordinating fabric.

Pink Monogram Chair

Paint the chair light pink. Choose a monogram letter from the alphabet on page 154. Sizing as needed to fit the chairback, make a photocopy of the letter. Decorate the letter with colored pencils, then use découpage glue to attach it to the chair; seal the surface with the glue. Cover the seat with fabric.

Green Monogram Chair

Paint a wooden chair green, then glue an iron-on monogram to the chairback. Use narrow ribbon to tie two large cream buttons to the slats of the chair.

Scatter a single layer of buttons over the seat, then mix and pour clear resin over them — use a wooden spoon to spread the coating evenly, taking it to the edges of the chair.

Tip: Shop for a chair with an indented seat to avoid having the poured resin run off the edges of the seat.

Time After Time
Page 57

Rose Clock Table

Spray paint the tray and stand gold. Paint the inside bottom of the tray with light green acrylic paint. Brush on a fruitwood gel stain and wipe off the excess to create an aged effect. Highlight with a metallic gold rub-on finish.

Adjusting the size to fit, photocopy the clock face on page 157. Drill a hole through the center of the tray to fit the clock module. Coat the bottom of the tray with découpage glue, then adhere the face to the tray, smoothing out any bubbles. When the glue is dry, seal the surface of the face with another coat of glue.

Attach a clock movement kit and hands large enough to fit the clock face. Apply self-adhesive numerals to mark the time. Top off the table with a round polished-edge glass piece.

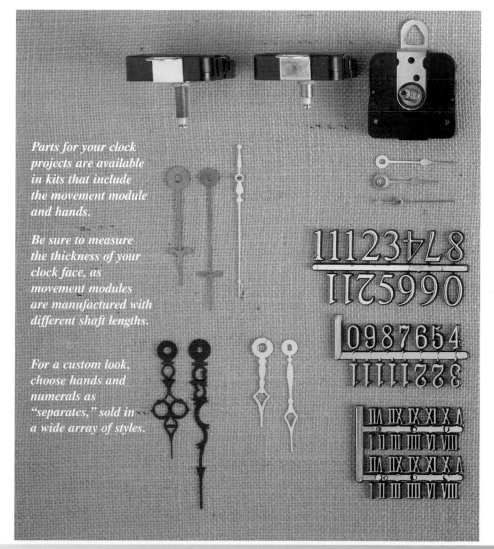

Parts for your clock projects are available in kits that include the movement module and hands.

Be sure to measure the thickness of your clock face, as movement modules are manufactured with different shaft lengths.

For a custom look, choose hands and numerals as "separates," sold in a wide array of styles.

A Time and a Season
Page 60

Clock Chalkboard

Remove a cardboard print from its frame, spray it with gray primer, then apply two or three coats of black chalkboard paint.

Sizing as needed to fit the top of the board, make a photocopy of the clock face on page 156. Use spray adhesive to adhere the face to the board, drill a hole through the center of the clock, then install a clock movement module and hands. Replace the board in the frame.

To separate the clock from the chalkboard, paint a thin piece of wooden trim to match the frame and glue it below the bottom edge of the clock face.

Page 61

Easel Clock

Paint an easel frame with green acrylic paint, then apply a fruitwood gel stain with a cloth, wiping off the excess. Use a gold metallic rub-on finish to accent the frame. Cut a piece of mat board to fit in the frame ... use spray adhesive to adhere an old print to the board for the clock face. Drill a hole through the clock face, then install a clock movement module and hands, adhere self-adhesive numerals, to the clock face, and secure it in the frame.

Tip: We applied black acrylic paint to the frame's finials, and to our clock hands and numerals, softening the bright gold so they stand out against our print — wipe off the excess paint to reveal the gold underneath.

Sweet Romance
Page 70

Hanging Sugar Bowl Candles

A lid-less sugar bowl becomes a candleholder by re-threading a necklace with a length of wire. (To avoid heat damage

from the candle's flame, leave a gap in the beads at the top of the hanger by cutting the wire longer than your necklace.) Wrap the wire ends around the handles, twisting it around itself to secure in place. Place a tea light or small votive candle in the sugar bowl.

Aged to Perfection
Page 76

Faux Marbleized Lamp

Apply a coat of primer over the entire lamp, excluding the socket. Paint the column with a light color paint. Use a dampened sea sponge to add a second color of paint — dab the sponge on a paper towel to remove excess paint. Use a pouncing motion to apply the paint (changing the position of the sponge every few presses), and allow some of the basecoat color to show through. Repeat this process with two darker shades of paint. If needed, repeat with the lighter colors over the darker ones to soften the marbling.

Paint the base black, then use a cloth to apply a metallic gold rub-on finish along the raised edges of the entire lamp base for highlights.

Page 79

Winning Metals
Page 78

"Bronze" Planter

Prime a brass planter inside and out and follow with a brown basecoat. Apply a coat of Fragile Crackle™ over the basecoat. Apply a black gel stain over the crackled surface, then lightly wipe away the excess. Sponge a mixture of light brown paint thinned with water on the surface of the planter. Apply a metallic gold rub-on finish along the rim and raised edges of the planter.

"Verdigris" Planter

For the look of aged copper, begin with a coat of primer followed by a pale olive-green basecoat. Lightly sponge dark green acrylic paint over the surface, allowing some of the basecoat to show through.

Brush on brown gel stain and use a soft cloth to wipe away the excess, allowing the colors underneath to show through. Apply a metallic gold rub-on finish along the rims and raised edges of the planter.

"Pewter" Container

Prime the container and follow with a flat black basecoat. To accentuate the hammered texture of the container use a wide angled brush to dry brush a metallic silver rub-on finish over the surface. To add depth, lightly dry brush the container with an antique gold rub-on finish.

Sweetness and Light
Page 81

Framed Sconce

Cut a piece of foam core board to fit inside a wooden frame for the backing, then cover the board with fabric.

Prime, then paint a brass candle sconce with acrylic paint. To make the holes to attach the sconce to the board, position the sconce on the backing, and mark each side of the sconce in two places. Remove the sconce and punch a hole at each mark. Place the sconce on the backing. Threading lengths of ribbon through the holes and around the sconce, thread one ribbon from front to back and knot ribbon ends at back, then thread the other ribbon from back to front and tie ends into a bow. Hot glue the board in the frame.

Removing the base from a candlestick lamp, hot glue the candlestick piece into the sconce. Refer to the four easy steps on this page to cover the shade and add trim.

4 easy steps to a fabric-covered lampshade

Remove the paper cover from a self-adhesive shade and use the paper as your pattern, or make a paper pattern for your non-adhesive shade.

Pin the pattern to your fabric, then cut the fabric 1" outside the pattern edges on all sides.

Use thick craft glue to adhere decorative trim along the top and bottom edges.

Smooth the fabric piece around the shade and overlap the ends at the back. Trim the fabric even with the top and bottom edges of the shade. If your shade is not self-adhesive, use spray adhesive to attach the fabric piece.

Now your freshly covered shade is ready to shed new light on your revamped lamp.

Tip: Place the pattern on your fabric so the best part of the design will be at the center front.

"Aged Tin" Lamp

To make a cover for an existing shade, simply follow our four easy steps, at right, to "age" embossed wallpaper. Use tracing paper to create a pattern for the shade's panels. Use the pattern to cut pieces of the painted wallpaper to fit each section of the shade and glue them in place. Glue braided trim along the seam lines and top and bottom edges of the shade.

Apply a rusting paint kit to the metal base of the lamp, then dry brush with antique white paint to complete the weathered look.

Paint a piece of dimensional wallpaper with rust-colored acrylic paint and allow to dry.

Apply a coat of cream acrylic paint over the rust and allow to dry.

Lightly sand wallpaper to reveal spots of the underlying rust color.

Apply a coat of spray varnish, letting spray accumulate in some areas to create an aged look.

Polka-Dot Pitcher Lamp

Hot glue plastic foam in the pitcher to add height ... glue a candlestick lamp to the foam. Add foam around the lamp, cover it with Spanish moss and insert a sprig of cherries. Top the lamp with a shade sponge-painted with blue acrylic paint.

Coffee Jar Lamp

To make the raised lettering on a coffee jar more visible, dry brush over the words with black paint, then slip a piece of light-colored poster board cut to fit inside the jar. Fill the jar with coffee beans and add a jar lid lamp kit. Top the lamp with a shade sponge-painted with red acrylic paint.

Bottle Adapter Kits

Bottle adapter lamp kits come with three sizes of adapters designed to fit almost any narrow-necked bottle.

Candlestick Lamps

Candlestick lamps are available in battery powered or electric form. Remove the base of the battery-powered lamp to insert the "candle" into another holder, such as a sconce.

Display Lamp Kits

Display lamp kits have an unfinished wooden base which can be painted or stained. Assemble and add a collectible object, such as our decanter, for an instant decorator look.

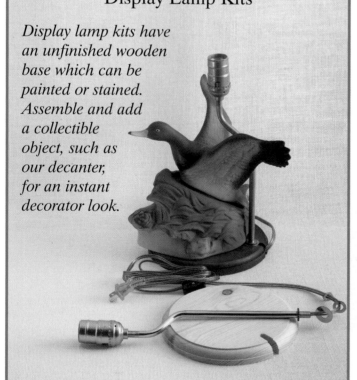

Basket Adapter Kits

Basket adapter kits have C-clamp style hardware, making it easy to convert items with a handle into lamps.

Romance of Candles
Page 106

Candle Chandeliers

Electric chandeliers are transformed into outdoor luminaries, by removing the lightbulbs, sockets, and wiring. Place tall glass votives with candles where the sockets once were, securing them in place with hot glue and plastic foam pieces. For outdoor hangers, use antiquing gel to create a vintage finish on iron shepherd's hooks.

A Light Aloft
Page 106-107

Hanging Candle Globes

If part of your metal shade is glass, like the amber glass on ours, take the globe apart to avoid getting paint on the glass.

Spray paint the inside of a metal light shade flat black. Spray the outside with gold metallic paint and sponge on multiple metallic acrylic paint colors for a layered finish. Reassemble your shade.

HANGING THE GLOBES

Thread a button onto the center of a generous length of

craft wire. Thread both ends of the wire through one of the shade's mounting holes from outside to inside, then thread as many beads as desired onto the wire. Repeat for each mounting hole, then twist all wire ends together at top. Bend the ends into a hanging loop, twisting the wire tightly around itself to secure. Hang the lamp on a shepherd's hook, then add a large candle or a large glass votive with a candle.

Baskets of Joy
Page 113

White-Washed Baskets

Prime and paint your baskets. Whitewash the baskets with a pickling stain, allowing some of the paint underneath to show through.

Playful Planters
Page 134-135

Polka-Dot Paint Trick

Paint a basecoat the desired color on the surface and allow to dry.

Randomly place ¾" round stickers on surface, pressing firmly to be sure the edges adhere.

Paint the surface with a second color and allow to dry.

Use the tip of a craft knife to carefully remove the stickers.

Apply two coats of sealer to the surface.

FLOUR

SUGAR

COFFEE

TEA

BREAD

ROLLS

COOKIES

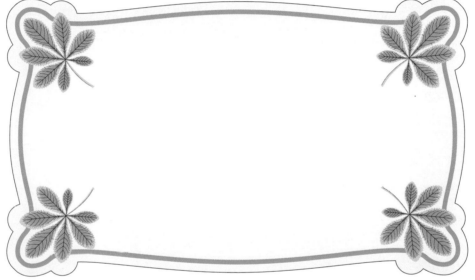

Field Lark.

ROSA
Centifolia cornea.

where to

find it...

Thank you Notes

Photography Stylist: Becky Charton
Photographer: Mark Mathews, The Peerless Group, Little Rock, Arkansas

Our sincere appreciation goes to the following businesses for their contributions to this book: Argenta Antique Mall, 201 East Broadway, North Little Rock, Arkansas 72114; Benton Flea Market, 18325 Interstate 30, Benton, Arkansas 72015; Blue Suede Shoes Antique Mall, 22460 Interstate 30, Bryant, Arkansas 72022; Collector's Market, 22430 Interstate 30, Bryant, Arkansas 72089; The Empress of Little Rock Bed & Breakfast, 2120 South Louisiana, Little Rock, Arkansas 72206; and Fabulous Finds, 301 South Bowman Road, Little Rock, Arkansas 72211, and 2905 Cantrell Road, Little Rock, Arkansas 72202.

Our very special thanks goes to Kim Blaylock of The Furniture Medic in North Little Rock, Arkansas, for the fantastic furniture refinishing.

Thank you, Jim Chudy of Jim's Taxidermy in Hazen, Arkansas, for loaning us your prized fishing lure collection. And with great appreciation,

we thank Jim Cogdell for allowing us to photograph his beautiful antique automobile in one of the fine parks maintained by the Little Rock Parks and Recreation Department.

We would also like to extend a warm thank you to the generous people who allowed us to photograph in their homes: Carl & Monte Brunck; Sandra Cook; Debbie Denton; Billy Joe & Wynona Glaze; Mark, Chris, Tyler, Parker, & Jackson Ham; Shirley Held; Lindsey Huckabay; Frankie & Kelly McKay; Patrick & Charity Miller; Lynn Phelps; Ellison Poe; September Rew; Bob & Kay Seay; Judy Smith; and Jeanne Spencer.

And a special thanks goes to our friend, Carla Prysock, who allowed us to photograph her flea market booth and whose marvelous "playhouse" will inspire many to discover their own flea market style!